EAS
Cc

MW01264620

THE EFFORTLESS CHEF SERIES VIII

By
Chef Maggie Chow
Copyright © 2015 by Saxonberg Associates

Published by
BookSumo, a division of Saxonberg Associates
http://www.booksumo.com/

A GIFT FROM ME TO YOU...

I know you like cultural food. But what about Japanese Sushi?

Join my private mailing list of readers and get a copy of *Infinite Sushi: A Complete Set of Sushi and Japanese Recipes* by fellow BookSumo author Hashimoto Kazuma for FREE!

http://booksumo.com/easy-cupcake-cookbook/

Enjoy some of the best sushi available!

You will also receive updates about all my new books when they are free. So please show your support.

Also don't forget to like and subscribe on the social networks. I love meeting my readers. Links to all my profiles are below so please click and connect :)

Facebook

Twitter

INTRODUCTION

Welcome to *The Effortless Chef Series*! Thank you for taking the time to download the *Easy Cupcake Cookbook*. Come take a journey with me into the delights of easy cooking. The point of this cookbook and all my cookbooks is to exemplify the effortless nature of cooking simply.

In this book we focus on cupcakes. You will find that even though the recipes are simple, the taste of the dishes is quite amazing.

So will you join me in an adventure of simple cooking? If the answer is yes (and I hope it is) please consult the table of contents to find the dishes you are most interested in. Once you are ready jump right in and start cooking.

— Chef Maggie Chow

TABLE OF CONTENTS

NOTICE TO PRINT READERS:

Hey, because you purchased the print version of this book you are entitled to its original digital version for free by Amazon.

So when you have the time, please review your purchases, and download the Kindle version of this book.

You might enjoy consuming this book more in its original digital format.

;)

But, in any case, take care and enjoy reading in whatever format you choose!

LEGAL NOTES

EASY CUPCAKE COOKBOOK

FUN CUPCAKES

(TEQUILA BASED CUPCAKES)

Ingredients

1. 1 (15.25 ounce) package yellow cake mix (such as Betty Crocker)
2. 1/2 cup butter, melted
3. 3 eggs
4. 1/2 cup lime margarita mix (such as Jose Cuervo)
5. 1 egg yolk
6. 3/4 cup lemon-lime soda
7. 1 1/2 (1.5 fluid ounce) tequila (such as Jose Cuervo)

Directions

1. Preheat your oven to 325 degrees F and line muffin cups with wax paper.
2. Combine all the ingredients mentioned above in a large sized bowl very thoroughly and pour this mixture into the muffin cups.
3. Bake in the preheated oven for about 30 minutes or until a toothpick that is inserted in the cake comes out clean.

Serving: 24

Timing Information:

Preparation	Cooking	Total Time
15 mins	30 mins	45 mins □

Nutritional Information:

Calories	136 kcal
Carbohydrates	16 g
Cholesterol	42 mg
Fat	6.7 g
Fiber	0.2 g
Protein	1.7 g
Sodium	159 mg

* Percent Daily Values are based on a 2,000 calorie diet.
□

BUTTERFINGER CUPCAKES

Ingredients

1. 1 (18.25 ounce) packaged chocolate or yellow cake mix
2. 36 pieces Butterfinger Bites Candy, chopped, divided
3. 1 (12 ounce) container prepared chocolate or vanilla frosting

Directions

1. Preheat your oven to 350 degrees F and line muffin cups with wax paper.
2. Combine all the ingredients mentioned above in a large sized bowl very thoroughly after preparing the mixture according to the package instructions and pour this mixture into the muffin cups.
3. Bake in the preheated oven for about 25 minutes or until a toothpick that is inserted in the cake comes out clean and garnish with Butterfinger bites after letting it cool down.

Serving: 24

Timing Information:

Preparation	Cooking	Total Time
10 mins	15 mins	40 mins ☐

Nutritional Information:

Calories	187 kcal
Carbohydrates	30.9 g
Cholesterol	0 mg
Fat	7.4 g
Fiber	0.7 g
Protein	1.9 g
Sodium	223 mg

* Percent Daily Values are based on a 2,000 calorie diet.☐

CUPCAKE BROWNIES

Ingredients

1. 1 cup butter
2. 1 cup chocolate chips
3. 4 eggs
4. 1 1/2 cups white sugar
5. 1 cup all-purpose flour
6. 1 teaspoon vanilla extract

Direction

1. Preheat your oven to 325 degrees F and line muffin cups with wax paper.
2. Now melt down chocolate chips and butter in a pan while stirring regularly.
3. Whisk eggs and sugar together, then add flour and vanilla extract into this mixture.
4. Add chocolate mixture and pour this into the prepared muffin cups, filling only half.
5. Bake in the preheated oven for about 30 minutes or until a toothpick that is inserted in the cake comes out clean.

Serving: 12

Timing Information:

Preparation	Cooking	Total Time
15 mins	35 mins	40 mins

Nutritional Information:

Calories	213 kcal
Carbohydrates	24.2 g
Cholesterol	74 mg
Fat	11.6 g
Fiber	0.4 g
Protein	3.2 g
Sodium	289 mg

* Percent Daily Values are based on a 2,000 calorie diet.□

AMERICAN CUPCAKES

Ingredients

1. 1 (8 ounce) package cream cheese
2. 1/4 cup confectioners' sugar
3. 1 egg
4. 1 (6 ounce) package chocolate chips
5. 1 (18.25 ounce) package chocolate cake mix
6. 4 maraschino cherries
7. 4 milk chocolate candy kisses
8. 4 walnut halves
9. 1 (1.4 ounce) bar chocolate covered toffee bars, chopped
10. 1/8 cup raisins
11. 1/4 cup candy coated peanut butter pieces

Directions

1. Preheat your oven to 350 degrees F and line muffin cups with wax paper.
2. Whisk egg, cream cheese and sugar together very thoroughly and add some chocolate chips in the bowl and set aside.
3. Now prepare the cake mixture according to package directions and pour this mixture into the prepared muffin cups.
4. In center of each cup, pour in egg and cream cheese mix with cherries.
5. Bake in the preheated oven for about 30 minutes or until a toothpick that is inserted in the cake comes out clean.

Serving: 24

Timing Information:

Preparation	Cooking	Total Time
15 mins	30 mins	45 mins

Nutritional Information:

Calories	194 kcal
Carbohydrates	25.3 g
Cholesterol	19 mg
Fat	10.3 g
Fiber	1.1 g
Protein	2.9 g
Sodium	218 mg

* Percent Daily Values are based on a 2,000 calorie diet.

SIMPLY COMPLEX CUPCAKE

Ingredients

1. 10 tablespoons butter, room temperature
2. 3/4 cup white sugar
3. 3 eggs
4. 1 teaspoon strawberry extract
5. 1 3/4 cups self-rising flour
6. 1/4 teaspoon salt
7. 1/4 cup finely chopped fresh strawberries, drained

Directions

1. Preheat your oven to 325 degrees F and line muffin cups with wax paper.
2. Add eggs one by one in a mixture of sugar and butter.
3. Now add strawberry extract, flour, and salt into the mixture.
4. Blend the mixture evenly.
5. Pour this mixture into the muffin cups.
6. Bake in the preheated oven for about 25 minutes or until a toothpick that is inserted in the cake comes out clean.

Serving: 12

Timing Information:

Preparation	Cooking	Total Time
15 mins	20 mins	1 hr 35 mins

Nutritional Information:

Calories	218 kcal
Carbohydrates	26.4 g
Cholesterol	72 mg
Fat	11 g
Fiber	0.6 g
Protein	3.5 g
Sodium	366 mg

* Percent Daily Values are based on a 2,000 calorie diet.

SNOW BUNNY CUPCAKES

Ingredients

1. 2/3 cup butter, softened
2. 3/4 cup superfine sugar
3. 1 1/2 cup self-rising flour
4. 3 eggs
5. 1 teaspoon vanilla extract

Directions

1. Preheat your oven to 325 degrees F and line muffin cups with wax paper.
2. Add eggs one by one into a properly blended mixture of sugar and butter.
3. Now add vanilla and flour into it, and mix it thoroughly.
4. Pour this mixture into the muffin cups.
5. Bake in the preheated oven for about 20 minutes or until a toothpick that is inserted in the cake comes out clean.

Serving: 12

Timing Information:

Preparation	Cooking	Total Time
15 mins	20 mins	35 mins

Nutritional Information:

Calories	213 kcal
Carbohydrates	24.2 g
Cholesterol	74 mg
Fat	11.6 g
Fiber	0.4 g
Protein	3.2 g
Sodium	289 mg

* Percent Daily Values are based on a 2,000 calorie diet.
☐

CHOCO-CHOCO-CHOCO CUPCAKES

Ingredients

1. 1 1/3 cups all-purpose flour
2. 1/4 teaspoon baking soda
3. 2 teaspoons baking powder
4. 3/4 cup unsweetened cocoa powder
5. 1/8 teaspoon salt
6. 3 tablespoons butter, softened
7. 1 1/2 cups white sugar
8. 2 eggs
9. 3/4 teaspoon vanilla extract
10. 1 cup milk

Directions

1. Preheat your oven to 325 degrees F and line muffin cups with wax paper.
2. Combine baking soda, flour, cocoa, baking powder and salt.
3. In a separate bowl add eggs one by one in the properly blended mixture of sugar and butter.
4. Add vanilla, flour mixture and milk alternatively into it and mix it thoroughly.
5. Pour this mixture into the muffin cups and fill ¾ of the cup.
6. Bake in the preheated oven for about 17 minutes or until a toothpick that is inserted in the cake comes out clean.

Serving: 16

Timing Information:

Preparation	Cooking	Total Time
15 mins	15 mins	30 mins

Nutritional Information:

Calories	158 kcal
Carbohydrates	29.8 g
Cholesterol	30 mg
Fat	3.9 g
Fiber	1.6 g
Protein	3.2 g
Sodium	114 mg

* Percent Daily Values are based on a 2,000 calorie diet.

MARIAM'S FAVORITE BANANA CUPCAKES

Ingredients

1. 3 bananas, mashed
2. 1 cup white sugar
3. 2 eggs, lightly beaten
4. 3/4 cup vegetable oil
5. 2 cups all-purpose flour
6. 2 teaspoons baking soda
7. 3 tablespoons buttermilk
8. 1 cup chopped pecans(optional)
9. 1 cup confectioners' sugar, or as needed

Directions

1. Preheat your oven to 300 degrees F and line muffin cups with wax paper.
2. In a separate bowl add eggs one by one in the properly blended mixture of sugar and bananas.
3. Now whisk vegetable oil into the mix for about 2 minutes and add buttermilk, flour and baking powder while continuing to mix.
4. Also add pecans.
5. Pour this mixture into the muffin cups and fill ¾ of each cup.
6. Bake in the preheated oven for about 30 minutes or until a toothpick that is inserted in the cake comes out clean and also sprinkle some confectioner sugar on top of these cupcakes.

Serving: 14

Timing Information:

Preparation	Cooking	Total Time
15 mins	20 mins	35 mins

Nutritional Information:

Calories	346 kcal
Carbohydrates	43.9 g
Cholesterol	27 mg
Fat	18.3 g
Fiber	1.9 g
Protein	3.8 g
Sodium	194 mg

* Percent Daily Values are based on a 2,000 calorie diet.

PIRATE CUPCAKES

Ingredients

1. 1 1/2 cups all-purpose flour
2. 1 teaspoon baking soda
3. 1/4 cup unsweetened cocoa powder
4. 1/2 teaspoon salt
5. 1 cup white sugar
6. 1/3 cup vegetable oil
7. 1 cup water
8. 1 tablespoon vinegar
9. 1 teaspoon vanilla extract
10. 1 (8 ounce) package cream cheese, softened
11. 1 egg
12. 1/3 cup white sugar
13. 1/8 teaspoon salt
14. 1 cup miniature semisweet chocolate chips

Directions

1. Preheat your oven to 350 degrees F and line muffin cups with wax paper.
2. Combine baking soda, flour, cocoa, baking powder and salt.
3. In a separate bowl combine sugar, water, oil, vinegar and vanilla.
4. Now add that flour mixture into it and mix it properly.
5. Pour this mixture into the muffin cups and fill 1/3 of the cup with this mixture and the remaining cup with a mixture of cream cheese, salt, egg and sugar.

6. Bake in the preheated oven for about 25 minutes or until a toothpick that is inserted in the cake comes out clean.

Serving: 24

Timing Information:

Preparation	Cooking	Total Time
10 mins	20 mins	30 mins

Nutritional Information:

Calories	171 kcal
Carbohydrates	22.4 g
Cholesterol	18 mg
Fat	8.9 g
Fiber	0.9 g
Protein	2.3 g
Sodium	145 mg

* Percent Daily Values are based on a 2,000 calorie diet.

BLACK & WHITE CUPCAKES

(OREO BASED CUPCAKES)

Ingredients

1. 1 package (2-layer size) chocolate cake mix
2. 1 (8 ounce) package cream cheese, softened
3. 1 egg
4. 2 tablespoons white sugar
5. 48 Mini OREO Bite Size Cookies, divided
6. 1 1/2 cups thawed frozen whipped topping

Directions

1. Preheat your oven to 350 degrees F and line muffin cups with wax paper.
2. Prepare chocolate cake mixture according to package instructions
3. In a separate bowl combine cream cheese, sugar and eggs completely.
4. Fill half of the cup with the following mixtures: cake mixture, and the cream cheese based mixture.
5. Fill the remaining half with more cake mixture.
6. Bake in the preheated oven for about 22 minutes or until a toothpick that is inserted in the cake comes out clean.

Serving: 24

Timing Information:

Preparation	Cooking	Total Time
10 mins	9 mins	52 mins

Nutritional Information:

Calories	213 kcal
Carbohydrates	24.2 g
Cholesterol	74 mg
Fat	11.6 g
Fiber	0.4 g
Protein	3.2 g
Sodium	289 mg

* Percent Daily Values are based on a 2,000 calorie diet.
☐

CUPCAKES PECAN

Ingredients

1. cooking spray with flour
2. 1 cup chopped pecans
3. 1 cup packed brown sugar
4. 1/2 cup whole wheat flour
5. 2/3 cup melted butter
6. 2 eggs, beaten
7. 24 whole pecans

Directions

1. Preheat your oven to 325 degrees F and line muffin cups with wax paper.
2. Combine all the ingredients mentioned above in an appropriate bowl.
3. Pour this mixture into the muffin cups while placing one pecan in the center of each cup.
4. Bake in the preheated oven for about 18 minutes or until a toothpick that is inserted in the cake comes out clean.

Serving: 12

Timing Information:

Preparation	Cooking	Total Time
10 mins	20 mins	1 hr 30 mins

Nutritional Information:

Calories	273 kcal
Carbohydrates	23.4 g
Cholesterol	58 mg
Fat	19.9 g
Fiber	1.8 g
Protein	3 g
Sodium	90 mg

* Percent Daily Values are based on a 2,000 calorie diet.
☐

CHEESY CHERRY CUPCAKES

Ingredients

Crust:

1. 1 cup graham cracker crumbs
2. 3/4 cup butter, melted
3. 2 tablespoons white sugar

Filling:

1. 1 pound whipped cream cheese
2. 3/4 cup sugar
3. 2 eggs
4. 1 teaspoon vanilla extract

Topping:

1. 1 (21 ounce) can cherry pie filling

Directions

2. Preheat your oven to 350 degrees F and line muffin cups with wax paper.
3. Pour mixture of graham cracker crumbs, 2 tablespoons of sugar and melted butter into muffin cups.
4. Whisk cream cheese, vanilla extract and sugar until the required smoothness is achieved in a separate bowl.
5. Pour this mixture into the muffin cups.

6. Bake in the preheated oven for about 10 minutes or until a toothpick that is inserted in the cake comes out clean.

Serving: 24

Timing Information:

Preparation	Cooking	Total Time
15 mins	10 mins	55 mins

Nutritional Information:

Calories	182 kcal
Carbohydrates	17.9 g
Cholesterol	49 mg
Fat	11.9 g
Fiber	0.2 g
Protein	1.8 g
Sodium	152 mg

* Percent Daily Values are based on a 2,000 calorie diet.

JELLY CUPCAKES

(PALEO SAFE CUPCAKES)

Ingredients

1. 1/2 cup applesauce
2. 1/2 cup coconut oil, melted
3. 3 eggs
4. 3 tablespoons honey
5. 1 tablespoon vanilla extract
6. 1/2 cup coconut flour
7. 1/2 teaspoon salt
8. 1/4 teaspoon baking soda
9. 1 tablespoon almond milk, or as needed (optional)
10. 1/2 cup raspberry jam, or as needed

Directions

1. Preheat your oven to 350 degrees F and line muffin cups with wax paper.
2. Using a food processer, blend honey, apple sauce, eggs, vanilla extract and coconut oil.
3. After transferring this mixture into a large bowl, add baking soda, coconut flour and some salt.
4. Mix thoroughly and add almond milk if it is too thick.
5. Pour this mixture into the muffin cups and fill ¾ of the cup with this mixture and add raspberry jam over each cup.

6. Bake in the preheated oven for about 25 minutes or until a toothpick that is inserted in the cake comes out clean.

Serving: 12
Timing Information:

Preparation	Cooking	Total Time
15 mins	25 mins	40 mins

Nutritional Information:

Calories	197 kcal
Carbohydrates	21.7 g
Cholesterol	46 mg
Fat	11.6 g
Fiber	4.2 g
Protein	3 g
Sodium	142 mg

* Percent Daily Values are based on a 2,000 calorie diet.□

HALLOWEEN CUPCAKES

(PUMPKIN CUPCAKES I)

Ingredients

1. 1 (15 ounce) can pumpkin puree
2. 1 1/2 cups white sugar
3. 1 cup packed brown sugar
4. 1/2 cup butter-flavored shortening
5. 1/2 cup butter, softened
6. 1/4 cup whole milk
7. 1/4 cup vegetable oil
8. 4 eggs
9. 2 cups cake flour
10. 1/4 cup dry buttermilk powder
11. 1/4 cup cornstarch
12. 2 teaspoons pumpkin pie spice
13. 2 teaspoons baking powder
14. 1 teaspoon baking soda
15. 3/4 teaspoon salt

Directions

1. Preheat your oven to 325 degrees F and line muffin cups with wax paper.
2. Whisk pumpkin puree, brown sugar, shortening, butter, white sugar, milk, vegetable oil, and eggs in a bowl until the required smoothness is achieved.
3. In a separate bowl mix cake flour, cornstarch, pumpkin pie spice, baking powder, dry buttermilk powder, baking soda, and salt.

4. Now add this dry mixture into the pumpkin mixture and mix it thoroughly.
5. Pour this mixture into the muffin cups and fill 2/3 of the cup with this mixture.
6. Bake in the preheated oven for about 30 minutes or until a toothpick that is inserted in the cake comes out clean.
7. Let the cupcakes cool before serving.

Serving: 24

Timing Information:

Preparation	Cooking	Total Time
15 mins	30 mins	45 mins

Nutritional Information:

Calories	250 kcal
Carbohydrates	34.5 g
Cholesterol	42 mg
Fat	11.7 g
Fiber	0.8 g
Protein	2.8 g
Sodium	258 mg

* Percent Daily Values are based on a 2,000 calorie diet.

LEMONY CUPCAKES WITHOUT THE GLUTEN

Ingredients

1. 5/8 cup milk, at room temperature
2. 3 3/4 teaspoons lemon juice
3. 1/4 cup vegetable oil
4. 2 egg whites, room temperature
5. 2 lemons, zested
6. 1 1/2 teaspoons vanilla extract
7. 1 1/8 cups gluten-free flour (such as Jeanne's Gluten-Free All-Purpose Flour Mix; recipe in footnotes)
8. 3/4 cup white sugar
9. 2 teaspoons double-acting baking powder
10. 1/4 teaspoon salt

Directions

1. Preheat your oven to 325 degrees F and line muffin cups with wax paper.
2. Beat milk and lemon juice together before adding egg whites, vanilla extract, vegetable oil, and lemon zest.
3. Now add this into a mixture of gluten free baking flour, salt, sugar and baking powder.
4. Blend thoroughly with an electric mixer for about 2 minutes.
5. Pour this mixture into the muffin cups and fill 3/4 of the cup.

6. Bake in the preheated oven for about 20 minutes or until a toothpick that is inserted in the cake comes out clean.
7. Allow cupcakes to cool before serving.

Serving: 12

Timing Information:

Preparation	Cooking	Total Time
10 mins	20 mins	1 hr □

Nutritional Information:

Calories	100 kcal
Carbohydrates	13.6 g
Cholesterol	1 mg
Fat	4.8 g
Fiber	0.1 g
Protein	1 g
Sodium	144 mg

* Percent Daily Values are based on a 2,000 calorie diet.

□

FRENCH REVOLUTION CUPCAKES

Ingredients

1. 1 1/4 cups all-purpose flour
2. 2/3 cup milk
3. 1/2 cup yogurt
4. 1/2 cup white sugar
5. 1/2 cup butter, melted
6. 1/2 cup raisins
7. 1/3 cup dark brown sugar
8. 2 tablespoons maple syrup, or more to taste
9. 1 1/2 teaspoons vanilla extract
10. 1 teaspoon baking powder
11. 1 teaspoon ground cinnamon
12. 1/2 teaspoon baking soda
13. 1/2 teaspoon salt

Directions

1. Preheat your oven to 325 degrees F and line muffin cups with wax paper.
2. Combine all the ingredients mentioned above very thoroughly in a bowl until the required smoothness is achieved.
3. Pour this mixture into the muffin cups.
4. Bake in the preheated oven for about 25 minutes or until a toothpick that is inserted in the cake comes out clean.
5. Allow cupcakes to cool before serving.

Serving: 12

Timing Information:

Preparation	Cooking	Total Time
15 mins	20 mins	35 mins

Nutritional Information:

Calories	106 kcal
Carbohydrates	16.5 g
Cholesterol	11 mg
Fat	4.1 g
Fiber	0.3 g
Protein	1.3 g
Sodium	125 mg

* Percent Daily Values are based on a 2,000 calorie diet.

Autumn Cupcakes

(Pumpkin Cupcakes II)

Ingredients

1. 2/3 cup all-purpose flour
2. 2 teaspoons pumpkin pie spice
3. 1/4 teaspoon baking powder
4. 1/4 teaspoon baking soda
5. 1/4 teaspoon salt
6. 1 (15 ounce) can pumpkin puree
7. 3/4 cup evaporated milk
8. 3/4 cup white sugar
9. 2 eggs
10. 1 teaspoon vanilla extract

Directions

1. Preheat your oven to 350 degrees F and line muffin cups with wax paper.
2. Whisk pumpkin puree, sugar, evaporated milk, white sugar, vanilla extract and eggs in a bowl until the required smoothness is achieved.
3. In a separate bowl mix cake flour, cornstarch, pumpkin pie spice, baking powder, dry buttermilk powder, baking soda, and salt.
4. Now add this dry mixture into the pumpkin mixture and mix it thoroughly.
5. Pour this mixture into the muffin cups and fill 1/3 of the cup with this mixture.

6. Bake in the preheated oven for about 20 minutes or until a toothpick that is inserted in the cake comes out clean.
7. Allow cupcakes to cool before serving.

Serving: 12
Timing Information:

Preparation	Cooking	Total Time
15 mins	20 mins	1 hr 35 mins

Nutritional Information:

Calories	121 kcal
Carbohydrates	22.6 g
Cholesterol	36 mg
Fat	2.2 g
Fiber	1.3 g
Protein	3.2 g
Sodium	199 mg

* Percent Daily Values are based on a 2,000 calorie diet.

FRUIT CUPCAKES

Ingredients

1. 1 (18.25 ounce) package white cake mix
2. 1 cup water
3. 1/3 cup vegetable oil
4. 3 eggs
5. 4 (0.13 ounce) package sweetened fruit-flavored drink mix (such as Kool-Aid)

Directions

1. Preheat your oven to 350 degrees F and line muffin cups with wax paper.
2. Combine all the ingredients mentioned above very thoroughly until required form is achieved.
3. Pour this mixture into the muffin cups and fill 2/3 of the cup with this mixture.
4. Bake in the preheated oven for about 15 minutes or until a toothpick that is inserted in the cake comes out clean.
5. Allow cupcakes to cool before serving.

Serving: 48

Timing Information:

Preparation	Cooking	Total Time
15 mins	15 mins	1 hr

Nutritional Information:

Calories	63 kcal
Carbohydrates	8.3 g
Cholesterol	12 mg
Fat	3 g
Fiber	0.1 g
Protein	0.9 g
Sodium	80 mg

* Percent Daily Values are based on a 2,000 calorie diet.

LEMONY CUPCAKES II

Ingredients

1. 1 package (2-layer size) white cake mix
2. 1 pkg. (4 serving size) Jell-O Lemon Instant Pudding
3. 1 cup water
4. 4 egg whites
5. 2 tablespoons oil
6. 3 3/4 cups icing sugar
7. 1 (250 g) package Philadelphia Light Brick Cream Cheese, softened
8. 1/4 cup butter, softened
9. 2 tablespoons lemon juice

Directions

1. Preheat your oven to 350 degrees F and line muffin cups with wax paper.
2. Mix all the ingredients mentioned above using an electric mixer at low speed for the first few minutes and at medium speed for two more minutes.
3. Pour this mixture into the muffin cups.
4. Bake in the preheated oven for about 24 minutes or until a toothpick that is inserted in the cake comes out clean.
5. Allow cupcakes to cool before serving.

Serving: 24

Timing Information:

Preparation	Cooking	Total Time
10 mins	25 mins	1 hr 35 mins

Nutritional Information:

Calories	235 kcal
Carbohydrates	40.9 g
Cholesterol	10 mg
Fat	7 g
Fiber	0.2 g
Protein	2.6 g
Sodium	265 mg

* Percent Daily Values are based on a 2,000 calorie diet.

EASY RED VELVET CUPCAKES

Ingredients

1. 1 package Red Velvet Cake Mix
2. 1 1/4 cups water
3. 1/3 cup vegetable oil
4. 3 large eggs
5. 1 (16 ounce) container Duncan Hines Creamy Home-Style Cream Cheese Frosting
6. Sprinkles or additional garnishes

Directions

1. Preheat your oven to 350 degrees F and line muffin cups with wax paper.
2. Mix all the ingredients mentioned above using an electric mixer at low speed for the first few minutes and at medium speed for two more minutes.
3. Pour this mixture into the muffin cups.
4. Bake in the preheated oven for about 22 minutes or until a toothpick that is inserted in the cake comes out clean.
5. Allow cupcakes to cool before serving.

Serving: 12

Timing Information:

Preparation	Cooking	Total Time
15 mins	20 mins	1 hr 10 mins

Nutritional Information:

Calories	203 kcal
Carbohydrates	30.2 g
Cholesterol	23 mg
Fat	9 g
Fiber	0.5 g
Protein	1.8 g
Sodium	177 mg

* Percent Daily Values are based on a 2,000 calorie diet.

CHOCOLATE CUPCAKES

Ingredients

1. 3/4 cup all-purpose flour
2. 3/4 cup white sugar
3. 3 tablespoons cocoa powder, or more to taste
4. 1/2 teaspoon baking powder
5. 3 tablespoons margarine, softened
6. 3 tablespoons water
7. 1/2 egg
8. 3 1/2 teaspoons vanilla extract
9. 6 milk chocolate candy kisses (such as Hershey's Kisses)

Directions

1. Preheat your oven to 350 degrees F and line muffin cups with wax paper.
2. Combine baking powder, flour, cocoa powder and sugar in a bowl very thoroughly.
3. Now add this into a mixture of vanilla extract, margarine, egg, and water.
4. Pour this mixture into the muffin cups, filling only half.
5. Also add a candy kiss into the center of each cup.
6. Bake in the preheated oven for about 25 minutes or until a toothpick that is inserted in the cake comes out clean.
7. Allow cupcakes to cool before serving.

Serving: 6

Timing Information:

Preparation	Cooking	Total Time
15 mins	20 mins	35 mins

Nutritional Information:

Calories	245 kcal
Carbohydrates	41.7 g
Cholesterol	17 mg
Fat	7.7 g
Fiber	1.5 g
Protein	3.1 g
Sodium	114 mg

* Percent Daily Values are based on a 2,000 calorie diet.

CHEESE CAKE CUPS II

Ingredients

1. 16 vanilla wafer cookies
2. 2 (8 ounce) packages cream cheese, softened
3. 3/4 cup white sugar
4. 2 eggs
5. 1 teaspoon vanilla extract

Directions

1. Preheat your oven to 350 degrees F and line muffin cups with wax paper.
2. Combine cream cheese, eggs, sugar and vanilla until the required smoothness is achieved.
3. Now pour this mixture into the baking cup after placing a wafer cookie at the bottom.
4. Bake in the preheated oven for about 15 minutes or until a toothpick that is inserted in the cake comes out clean.
5. Allow cupcakes to cool before serving.

Serving: 16

Timing Information:

Preparation	Cooking	Total Time
15 mins	15 mins	30 mins

Nutritional Information:

Calories	172 kcal
Carbohydrates	14.5 g
Cholesterol	54 mg
Fat	11.5 g
Fiber	0.1 g
Protein	3.2 g
Sodium	110 mg

* Percent Daily Values are based on a 2,000 calorie diet.

VANILLA CHEESECAKES II

Ingredients

1. 12 paper baking cups (2-1/2-inch)
2. 12 vanilla wafers
3. 1 (8 ounce) package cream cheese, softened
4. 2 tablespoons sugar
5. 1 tablespoon Argo Corn Starch
6. 1 egg
7. 1/3 cup Karo Light Corn Syrup
8. 1 tablespoon lemon juice
9. 1 teaspoon Spice Islands Pure Vanilla Extract
10. Fresh fruit, jam, pie filling or chocolate curls

Directions

1. Preheat your oven to 350 degrees F and line muffin cups with wax paper.
2. Combine cream cheese, eggs, sugar, corn syrup and lemon juice using an electric mixer at low speed for about 3 minutes or until the required smoothness is achieved.
3. Now pour this in the baking cup after placing a vanilla wafer.
4. Bake in the preheated oven for about 20 minutes or until a toothpick that is inserted in the cake comes out clean.
5. Allow cupcakes to cool before serving.

Serving: 12

Timing Information:

Preparation	Cooking	Total Time
15 mins	20 mins	1 hr 35 mins

Nutritional Information:

Calories	143 kcal
Carbohydrates	15.6 g
Cholesterol	36 mg
Fat	8.2 g
Fiber	0.3 g
Protein	8.9 g
Sodium	89 mg

* Percent Daily Values are based on a 2,000 calorie diet.

☐

CHERRY CHEESECAKES CUPCAKES II

Ingredients

1. 24 vanilla wafer cookies
2. 2 (8 ounce) packages cream cheese, softened
3. 3/4 cup white sugar
4. 2 eggs
5. 2 1/2 tablespoons lemon juice
6. 1 teaspoon vanilla extract
7. 1 (12 ounce) can cherry pie filling

Directions

1. Preheat your oven to 350 degrees F and line muffin cups with wax paper.
2. Combine cream cheese, eggs, sugar, vanilla extract and lemon juice using an electric mixer at low speed for about 3 minutes or until the required smoothness is achieved.
3. Now pour this mixture in the baking cup after placing a vanilla wafer at the bottom, filling 2/3 of the cup.
4. Bake in the preheated oven for about 20 minutes or until a toothpick that is inserted in the cake comes out clean
5. Cool it down and place cherries on every cupcake before serving.

Serving: 24

Timing Information:

Preparation	Cooking	Total Time
15 mins	15 mins	2 hr

Nutritional Information:

Calories	141 kcal
Carbohydrates	15.1 g
Cholesterol	36 mg
Fat	8.1 g
Fiber	0.2 g
Protein	2.2 g
Sodium	82 mg

* Percent Daily Values are based on a 2,000 calorie diet.

Chocolate Cupcakes Without the Gluten

Ingredients

1. 1 1/2 cups white rice flour
2. 3/4 cup millet flour
3. 1/2 cup unsweetened cocoa powder
4. 1 teaspoon salt
5. 1 teaspoon baking soda
6. 1 tablespoon baking powder
7. 1 teaspoon xanthan gum
8. 4 eggs
9. 1 1/4 cups white sugar
10. 2/3 cup sour cream
11. 1 cup milk
12. 2 teaspoons vanilla extract

Directions

1. Preheat your oven to 350 degrees F and line muffin cups with wax paper.
2. Combine rice flour, xanthan gum, millet flour, cocoa, baking powder, salt and baking soda very thoroughly.
3. Whisk eggs, vanilla, sugar, milk and sour cream together in a separate bowl.
4. Now add the dry mixture with the wet mixture and mix until the required smoothness is achieved.
5. Pour this mixture into the muffin cups.

6. Bake in the preheated oven for about 25 minutes or until a toothpick that is inserted in the cake comes out clean.
7. Allow cupcakes to cool before serving.

Serving: 24

Timing Information:

Preparation	Cooking	Total Time
15 mins	20 mins	35 mins

Nutritional Information:

Calories	130 kcal
Carbohydrates	23.8 g
Cholesterol	35 mg
Fat	2.9 g
Fiber	1.4 g
Protein	3 g
Sodium	235 mg

* Percent Daily Values are based on a 2,000 calorie diet.

A GIFT FROM ME TO YOU...

I know you like cultural food. But what about Japanese Sushi?

Join my private mailing list of readers and get a copy of *Infinite Sushi: A Complete Set of Sushi and Japanese Recipes* by fellow BookSumo author Hashimoto Kazuma for FREE!

http://booksumo.com/easy-cupcake-cookbook/

Enjoy some of the best sushi available!

You will also receive updates about all my new books when they are free. So please show your support.

Also don't forget to like and subscribe on the social networks. I love meeting my readers. Links to all my profiles are below so please click and connect :)

Facebook

Twitter

COME ON...
LET'S BE FRIENDS :)

I adore my readers and love connecting with them socially. Please follow the links below so we can connect on Facebook, Twitter, and Google+.

Facebook

Twitter

I also have a blog that I regularly update for my readers so check it out below.

My Blog

ABOUT THE PUBLISHER.

BookSumo specializes in providing the best books on special topics that you care about. *The Easy Cupcake Cookbook* focuses on the simplest and most amazing cupcake recipes.

To find out more about BookSumo and find other books we have written go to:

http://booksumo.com/.

CAN I ASK A FAVOUR?

If you found this book interesting, or have otherwise found any benefit in it. Then may I ask that you post a review of it on Amazon? Nothing excites me more than new reviews, especially reviews which suggest new topics for writing. I do read all reviews and I always factor feedback into my newer works.

So if you are willing to take ten minutes to write what you sincerely thought about this book then please visit our Amazon page and post your opinions.

Again thank you!

INTERESTED IN OTHER EASY COOKBOOKS?

Everything is easy check out some of my other cookbooks:

Grilling:

Easy Grilling Cookbook

Smoothies:

Easy Smoothie Cookbook

Nutella

Easy Nutella Cookbook

Filipino Cuisine:

Easy Filipino Cookbook

Quiche:

Easy Quiche Cookbook

Burgers:

Easy Burger Cookbook

Made in the USA
Lexington, KY
27 July 2015